C000040066

MONMOUTH
AND
THE RIVER WYE
IN OLD PHOTOGRAPHS
FROM GOODRICH TO BROCKWEIR

MONMOUTH
AND
THE RIVER WYE
IN OLD PHOTOGRAPHS
FROM GOODRICH TO BROCKWEIR

—FROM THE COLLECTIONS OF—
MONMOUTH MUSEUM

———— COMPILED BY ————
ANDREW HELME

ALAN SUTTON
1989

Alan Sutton Publishing
Gloucester

First published 1989

British Library Cataloguing in Publication Data

Around Monmouth in old photographs.
1. Gwent. Monmouth (District). Lower Wye Valley. Villages, history
I. Helme, Andrew
942.9'98

ISBN 0-86299-481-0

Front cover illustration
MONMOUTH and the River Wye, c. 1870. (See page 40.)

Typesetting and origination by
Alan Sutton Publishing
Printed in Great Britain by
Dotesios Printers Limited

CONTENTS

MONNOW BRIDGE, c. 1925, taken by W.A. Call (see page 71).

INTRODUCTION

Monmouth is the main subject of the photographs in this book, with short excursions up and down the River Wye as far as Goodrich Castle and Brockweir. The photographs are arranged according to place, and no attempt has been made to provide a pictorial chronological history. The pictures date mainly from the late-nineteenth century and the first three decades of the twentieth, with several earlier and later. The latest was taken in 1963, but this is an exception, and the period since the Second World War has, in the main, been left for some future publication.

All the photographs are from the collections of Monmouth Museum, except for 13 from Chepstow Museum (see the list on page 9). The decision to select entirely from the museum holdings was based on the desire to make the collection, which at Monmouth contains over 4,000 photographs, better known and more access-ible. The underlying hope also exists that local people will be encouraged to deposit more photographs and information in the museum, for even with so many images already preserved, there are many gaps in the coverage of the town and neighbouring areas. Some gaps may be obvious in this book: we have very few photographs of the interior of buildings, public or private (other than the Rolls Hall!), or of people at work; certain areas of the town away from the main streets are sparsely covered, if at all. Of course, the collection is constantly being added to, and no lower age limit is placed upon new arrivals – yesterday is old enough.

The measures taken to preserve photographs in the care of the museum are growing more and more complex. Over recent years it has become increasingly clear that the photographic image is one of the most fragile types of object with which we deal. Stable, dry, cool and dark conditions are essential to avoid deterioration of the image in the long-term and handling of prints is kept to a minimum. The use of the copy prints for reference and display purposes is becoming standard practice, and the appeal for old photographs to be given to the museum is based, as much upon the need to ensure the preservation of the photograph as an object, as upon the need to record the information it contains. It is usually possible to provide good quality copy prints in exchange for old photographs with high intrinsic personal or family value.

Photographs are practically useless without the information which puts them into context. The *Monmouthshire Beacon* newspaper has been used extensively to identify and provide background information about the people, events and places shown here. Use of the *Beacon* has been made much easier by the work of Keith Kissack, who first indexed the pre-1914 issues and then produced *Victorian Monmouth* (1986), a detailed history of the town from the 1830s to the First World War based upon the reports and opinions expressed in the *Beacon* and the shorter-lived local papers, the *Merlin* and the *Gazette*. Keith Kissack has also been unstinting in his response to many direct appeals for information.

Much basic identification work on many of the photographs in the museum was carried out as part of a Community Enterprise project to catalogue the collection, particularly by Mrs P.J. Shaw over two years from March 1984, when known information was recorded and new detail researched. More information has been added during the compilation of the book, usually directly from individual members of the public, often the photograph donors (listed on page 160) or knowledgeable past and present residents. Mr Stan Coates, Mrs Audrey Kissack, Miss Betty Williams, Miss Iris Williams, Mrs N. Steen (née Call), and Mr Derek Jones are some of those who have given particular help. Mrs Sue Miles and Margaret Colin of Monmouth Museum have assisted with searches of the *Beacon* and with general support during compilation.

BIBLIOGRAPHY

The following books have been used during compilation:

Coates, S.C. & Tucker, D.G., *Watermills of the Monnow and Trothy*. Monmouth, 1978.

Davies, E.T. & Kissack, K.E., *The Inns and Friendly Societies of Monmouth*. Monmouth, 1981.

Harris, P.G., *Wye Valley Industrial History*. (Typescript in Monmouth Museum.)

Jones, R., *History of the Red Cross in Monmouthshire (Gwent) 1910–1918*. Pontypool, 1988.

Kissack, K.E., *The River Wye*. Monmouth, 1978.

Paar, H.W., *The Severn and Wye Railway*. Newtown Abbott, 1963.

Pevsner, N., *The Buildings of England: Herefordshire*. Harmondsworth, 1963.

Shirehampton, W.J.P., *Monmouth's Railways*. Monmouth, 1959.

Stanford, S.C., *The Archaeology of the Welsh Marches*. London, 1980.

MONMOUTH PHOTOGRAPHERS

Listed below are the page numbers and positions (t=top, b=bottom) on each page of photographs known to have been taken by local commercial photographers. The addresses and dates given are from trade directories and the photographs themselves.

W.A. Call, The County Studio, No. 3 Priory Street. (c. 1911 on. See page 71.)
p. 7; p. 11(b); p. 42(t & b); p. 55(t); p. 57(b); p. 62(b); p. 71(t, left & b); p. 89(t); p. 143(b); p. 159(t, right & b, both).

Archie L. Cranch, No. 6 Whitecross Street. (c. 1905 to 1926.)
p. 22; p. 27(t); p. 38(t); p. 69(t).

George F. Harris, No. 8 Monnow Street/1 Glendower Street. (c. 1902 to 1920.)
p. 10/11(t); p. 15(t & b); p. 18(t); p. 25(t); p. 27(b); p. 34; p. 51(t); p. 68; p. 81; p. 84(t); p. 85; p. 100(b); p. 123(t); p. 125(t).

Emil Henri du Heaume, No. 18, St James' Street. (c. 1929 to 1945.)
p. 58(b); p. 65; p. 69(b); p. 124(t); p. 149(b).

Charles Vickris Hyam, No. 33 Monnow Street. (c. 1910 to 1935.)
p. 39(t); p. 77(t & b); p. 103(b); p. 122(b); p. 123(b); p. 151.

John Howard Preston, No. 66 Monnow Street, (c. 1895 to 1907.)
p. 10(b); p. 16; p. 31; p. 50; p. 98; p. 99.

Richard Tudor Williams, No. 98 Monnow Street. (c. 1865 to 1900.)
p. 28; p. 29(t); p. 41(t); p. 52(t); p. 92(t); p. 111; p. 143(t).

The following photographs are from the collections of Chepstow Museum:

p. 120; p. 153(t & b); p. 155(t & b); p. 157(t & b); p. 158(t & b); p. 159(all).

MONMOUTH, THE GREAT FLOOD, 1910. In December, a week of high rivers ended in floods following a gale and heavy rain. Waves two – three ft high were seen at Chippenham and the lower part of the town was cut off. Sixty – seventy ft of the embankment of the Wye Valley railway were washed away. The two rivers continued to rise over the weekend, there were six feet of water at Chippenham and five feet in Dixton Church (see page 18). The photograph is divided into two and continues on the next page, top. In the foreground is the Redbrook Road. Wye Bridge is on the right of the picture.

ABOVE: MONMOUTH FROM THE SOUTH-EAST, the Wye and the two railway bridges in the foreground.

LEFT: A CLOSER VIEW from the same direction, with Monmouth School for Girls (1897) on the right, top. The riverside area of the town before alteration for the dual-carriageway of the A40 can be seen particularly well, especially the terraces of houses, warehouses and quays upstream (right) of the Wye Bridge.

MONMOUTH, c. 1950, (above and opposite) showing the riverside before the dual-carriageway, with Chippenham, top left, River Monnow, top right, and Old Dixton Road, bottom right.

NOTE THE UNDEVELOPED STATE OF MONMOUTH SCHOOL in the Almshouse Street/Wierhead Street/Chippenhamgate Street areas; and Granville Street running across the two pages from the end of the Wye Bridge.

MONMOUTH GAOL, Hereford Road, c. 1866. Opened in 1790, only the Gatehouse now remains. Built as a new County Gaol to the design of prison reformer John Howard, it was abandoned in 1869, its function transferred to Usk. The stone was eventually sold for building in Monmouth and at Sharpness Docks. Executions were carried out in public on the flat roof of the Gatehouse until at least 1859, when Mathew Francis was hanged for the murder of his wife. The Hospital was later built on part of the site. The other buildings shown are the toll-house and gate of the Monmouth to Llancloudy turnpike, established in 1755, the Herefordshire House pub and North Parade House beyond.

MEMBERS OF THE ROYAL ANCIENT ORDER OF BUFFALOES at the rear of Victoria Place, c. 1920. Back row, left to right: G. Brooks (publican, Three Horse Shoes), W. Mackie (builder), J. Smith (cinema owner), -?-, K.E. Smith (floorwalker, Ackland's shop). Middle: -?-, D. Morgan (builder), -?-, Price (printer), W. French (baker). Front: -?-, C. Curtis (publican, Angel Hotel), R. Mackie (clerk to Jarrett), C. Jarrett (bookmaker), E. Hayward (hairdresser), Cumbley (hairdresser), J. Morris, C. Perry (tailor), B. Morris (clerk to Jarrett. Son of J. above).

CONVALESCENT WOUNDED SOLDIERS, C. 1917. Monmouth Red Cross Auxiliary Hospital, Parade House, Hereford Road. The occasion for the photograph seems to have been a day trip (on the river – note the gramophone) organized by Mr Arnott, a benefactor of the Hospital, seen here (above) second left in the second row from the back. A total of 1,422 patients were treated between 1915 and 1919.

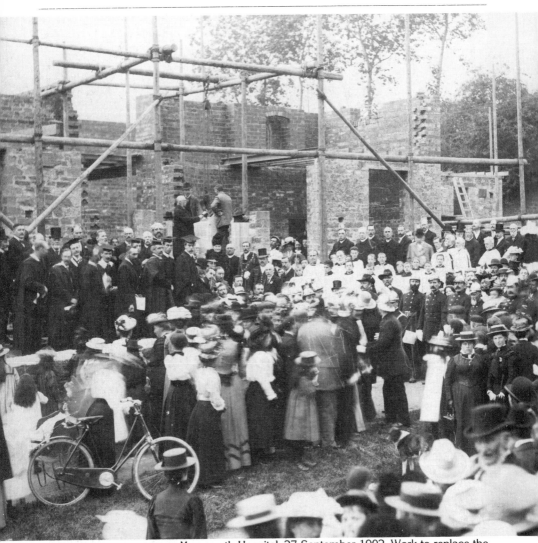

LAYING THE MEMORIAL STONE, Monmouth Hospital, 27 September 1902. Work to replace the old hospital, in St James' Square (see page 35), with a purpose-built one on the Hereford Road began in April 1902. Lord Llangattock, as President of the hospital and leading contributor to the building fund (£2,000) was invited to lay the memorial stone in the main entrance. The ceremony began at 3 p.m. with a procession from the old hospital, led by the Fire Brigade and including the Mayor (Hamilton T. Baillie) and Corporation, the Grammar School staff, honorary medical staff, Hospital Governors and subscribers. A crowd of 1,000 gathered at the site, swelled by the local clergy who arrived from the vicar's house nearby to conduct the service. In his address, Lord Llangattock reminded critics of the expense of the new building that it was 'for the suffering and afflicted poor'.

OPPOSITE: FURTHER STAGES IN THE COMPLETION OF THE HOSPITAL, which was opened on 6 November 1903, by Lord Llangattock.

ABOVE: THE INTERIOR OF DIXTON CHURCH, 1910, after the flood. Note the tide-mark on the wall. Water levels in the church have long been one of the standards used in comparing successive Monmouth floods.

BELOW: OLD DIXTON ROAD, 1910 flood. The buildings on the right have now all gone. William Walters, monumental-mason, had his work-yard behind the wall. At one time a lady known as 'Emma-smoke-a-pipe' lived in the house at the end of the wall.

DIXTON GATE, 1937/38, looking along the Old Dixton Road, the Turnpike cottage in the centre. The houses on the left have been replaced by the recent Burgage development.

MAKING A HAYSTACK, 1910. The individuals and the location have not yet been identified. The area between the old and new Dixton roads, now used by the Comprehensive School, is a possibility.

CROWNING THE MAY QUEEN, 8 June 1908. Lady Llangattock performed the crowning, seen here with the May Queen, Miss Marjorie Edwards, on the 'car' which later in the day won second prize for 'best group' in the Children's Pageant competition. The Pageant was organized to raise funds for the restoration of 'Geoffrey's Window' in the Priory, and took place on the sports field, Old Dixton Road, after a procession through the streets. (See page 101.) Events on the field included Maypole dancing by the Girls' School, sports competitions for children and adults, and pig-singing. This involved individuals in the rendition of a song while holding a struggling piglet under one arm. The prize (the pig) was won by Frank Collins of Monmouth. The pig was given by A.E. Jones of Troy Farm. The Pageant was billed as Monmouth's first Historical Pageant and the entries set the tone for many future events: Henry V on horseback; the Childhood of Henry V at Courtfield; the Grant of the Freedom of Monmouth to Lord Nelson; St George and the Dragon; the Grant of the First Charter to Monmouth by Henry VI. Following judging of the entries on the field by Lady Llangattock, Miss Bagnall-Oakeley and Mr Hobson-Mathews, tea was available either from the 'Café Chantant' tent at 1s., or from the 6d. tent. George Edwards, father of the May Queen and former mayor, is standing to the right of the steps. To the left is the Vicar of Monmouth, Revd C.F. Reeks.

MISS MARJORIE EDWARDS, Monmouth May Queen, 1908. During her crowning ceremony she was presented with a gold brooch from the children as a token of gratitude for the kindness of her father during his period as mayor.

ABOVE: THE SPORTS FIELD, Old Dixton Road, 8 June 1908, showing part of the crowd assembled for the Children's Pageant (see page 20).

TOP, RIGHT: COMING OF AGE CELEBRATION, Bernard Edwards, 1905, Little Chippenham. The photograph was taken by George F. Harris in the early evening of a day of entertainment provided for all the elementary schoolchildren of Monmouth by George Edwards, mayor, to celebrate his son's twenty-first birthday. Presentations had just been made by the children of a bouquet to Mrs Edwards and a silver inkstand to Bernard. Also on the platform are the vicar, Revd C.F. Reeks and B.H. Deakin, the town clerk. Earlier in the afternoon, tea had been provided between bouts of athletics, rides on Hill's roundabout and visits to Colbrook's Cinematograph, stationed in the Cattle Market along with sweet stalls. The day was started and finished with a procession through the town led by the RMRE(M) band, the children eventually being dispersed from the Market Hall with a bag of sweets and an orange each.

RIGHT: SPORTS ON DIXTON MEADOWS, c. 1905. August Bank Holiday sports were an annual event, and the 100-yard sprint final shown here was won by Tom 'Digger' Lewis, with Charles Wigmore second (see page 56), both well-known local athletes. The photograph was taken by Harry Hedger, another local sportsman.

23

ABOVE: IVY BANK, MONK STREET, 1 December 1941. Built in the 1730s, the classical embellishments which make the house so distinctive were added in the early 1800s. From c. 1909 to 1945 it was owned by Mr and Mrs Oliver Jones. Following the early death of Oliver, an auctioneer, in 1931, his wife, Ethel Annie, ran 'Ivy Bank' as a lodging house, (left, in 1935). She was Monmouth's first female mayor, in 1930, having been the first woman elected to the Council in 1921. She held many public offices, including Chairmanship of the Juvenile and County Benches, Governor of Monmouth School and the School for Girls, Alderman, and Chairman of the newly established Nelson Museum from 1925. She died on 5 February 1952.

TOP, RIGHT: THE WEDDING OF ETHEL ANNIE TEAGUE AND OLIVER LEOPOLD JONES, 22 April 1909. Ethel Annie's parents lived near Coleford, where the photograph was taken. The bridesmaids were her sisters, from left to right: Dora, Grace, Olive and May.

MONMOUTH MARKET, 12 September 1919. Oliver Jones, of Rennie and Jones, presiding at the Great Sheep Sale.

FOUNDATION CEREMONY, Monmouth Baptist Church, 3 January 1907. Three foundation stones were laid in the outer wall of the entrance porch by Miss Friend of Hereford, Mr W. Edwards of Newport, President of the Monmouthshire English Baptist Association, and by M.W. Sambrook of Wyesham, Secretary of the Monmouth Baptist Church. Each stone represented a major contribution to the building fund, Miss Friend's from her family, Mr Edwards' from the Baptist Union of Great Britain and Ireland, and Mr Sambrook's his own personal contribution.

TOP, RIGHT: THE SITE OF THE NEW BAPTIST CHURCH, Monk Street, showing the buildings acquired to make the project possible. The house in the centre was demolished, the one on the left turned into the Manse. The Working Men's Institute is on the right.

RIGHT: THE NEW CHURCH was opened on 17 October 1907, an occasion preceded by a public luncheon in the Working Men's Institute and followed by tea there as well. At the luncheon, Mr Sambrook reported that £1,238 10s. was owed on the new church. During the opening day and at the first Sunday service, £226 12s. 5d. were collected towards the cost. The new church replaced the original building of 1818, off Monnow Street.

Opening New Baptist Church, Monmouth. 17-10-07.

THE OPENING OF THE ROLLS HALL, 24 May 1888. The Hall was built as a gift to the town by John Allan Rolls of the Hendre, to commemorate the Golden Jubilee of Queen Victoria's reign. In his speech at the opening, he said: 'You will all agree with me that for a number of years we have all felt the inconvenience of the public hall with which this town has been provided,' (the Borough Court, Shire Hall, currently the County Library) 'I have long been wishing to give something to the good people of Monmouth . . . that would really be useful to them . . . I hope that (the Hall) will be useful to all classes, not only for amusement, but for instruction and for improving and enlarging the minds of our younger generation in Monmouth'. The Deed of Gift stated that the Hall was given to the Burgesses of Monmouth without any monetary consideration whatsoever, the only stipulation being that the Hall should not be used 'for any purpose hostile to the Church of England or the Throne of the realm'. In response, the town clerk read an address from the Council which ended; 'In offering you our heartfelt thanks for this costly gift we trust that in honour of the generous donor you will permit us to name it the Rolls Hall.' (*Beacon*, 26 May 1888.) The photograph shows J.A. Rolls, with his wife, Georgiana, on the stage having received the illuminated address from the mayor, George Higgins (front, left). To the left of the stage are members of 'C' Company, 4th Volunteer Battalion of the South Wales Borderers, who had formed a Guard of Honour outside the Hall. On the right are members of the band of the RMEM, which led the procession to the Hall.

LORD LLANGATTOCK, as Mayor of Monmouth, 1896–8. John Allan Rolls was born on 19 February 1837 and died on 24 September 1912. He married Georgiana Marcia Maclean in 1868 and was created the first Baron Llangattock in 1892. He was elected Conservative MP for Monmouthshire in 1880, but failed to secure re-election in 1885 and 1892. He founded the Rolls Habitation of the Primrose League in 1884. As a Freemason, he was elected Worshipful Master of the Loyal Monmouth Lodge in 1910. As local 'squire', he and his family were great benefactors of Monmouth, as several of the photographs in this book illustrate.

JOHN MACLEAN ROLLS as Mayor of Monmouth, 1906–7. He was born in April 1870 and was killed in action in Flanders in November 1916. He worked as a barrister and, in 1900, was High Sherriff of the County. He became the second Baron Llangattock on the death of his father in 1912. He went to war with the 1st Monmouthshire Artillery, 4th Welsh Brigade, in October 1916 and was mortally wounded about three weeks later. He died in a military hospital in Boulogne, with his mother and sister at his bedside. The Lordship ended with him, both his brothers, Charles and Henry, having already died.

MASONIC MEETING, Rolls Hall, c. 1905. The two banners on either side of the stage are of the 'Loyal Monmouth Lodge' and the 'Silurian Lodge', but the reason for the meeting is so far unknown and the identity of most of those present has yet to be established. Lord Llangattock is standing at the front of the stage on the chairman's left.

ART AND CRAFTS EXHIBITION, Rolls Hall, 25–28 October 1899. Organized by Lady Llangattock, the exhibition was intended to show and promote the arts and 'industries' of Wales and Monmouthshire. The amazing jumble of goods was divided into competitive and non-competitive exhibits, the latter gathered from sources such as the South Kensington Museum, the Duke of Beaufort and the Llangattocks themselves, who provided a selection from their growing collection of Nelson memorabilia. A large table in the centre of the hall, shown in the photograph, was reserved for the competitive exhibits, which were grouped according to county. The end nearest the stage, in the foreground of the photograph, was occupied by the Glamorganshire entries, which included pottery from Ewenny; shawls, tweeds and blankets from Bargoed; knitted goods from the Blind School in Cardiff; and a cloth called 'Rami', a mixture of wool and thread. In the gallery, two lady palmists were installed in gypsy tents, Miss Howells of Carmarthenshire and Miss Alice Smith of Leominster.

WHITECROSS STREET, c. 1925. The porch was not an original feature of the Rolls Hall, and has recently been removed except for the bases of the supporting columns.

TOP, RIGHT: THE MONMOUTH PIERROT ORCHESTRA, c. 1925, in the Rolls Hall. Left to right: Sydney Partridge, Steve Clark, Tristram Blay, Cyril Call, Rowley Call, Don Bennett, Howard Bowen.

MONMOUTH AMATEUR OPERATIC SOCIETY, *Iolanthe*, February 1925, Rolls Hall. Front (kneeling & sitting), left to right: -?-, -?-, Phyllis Morris, Mrs Barry (musical director), -?-, Evelyn Simmonds. Second row: N.C. Elstob (prompter), -?-, -?-, Gladys Park, -?-, -?-, A. Cotterill, Maud Morris, J.T. Vizard, Dolly Morgan, Mrs Vizard, F.C. Morgan, Phyllis Croudace, Charles Saunders, 'Toot' Simmonds, -?-, -?-, Bill Williams (stage manager), -?-, S.A. Herbert. Third row: Maud Redpath, Jean Redpath, -?-, -?-, -?-, -?-. Fourth row: -?-, S. Partridge, A.L. Barry, C. Croudace, Fred Pyner, -?-, -?-, -?-, C. Teague, Percy Hall. Back row: -?-, -?-, B. Partridge, -?-, L.T. Powell, Howard Bowen, George Beard, Reg Mackie.

ROLLS HALL INTERIOR, 18 July 1919, in readiness for the dinner given that evening to the demobilized and discharged men of Monmouth, over 500 of whom took part after marching through the town (see page 85). Monmouth's Peace Celebrations continued on the following day with processions, children's and adult sports, a ball and tea for the aged and the inmates of the Workhouse. The interior decorations of the Hall include notices prohibiting smoking, requesting the public to refrain from spitting and reminding audiences of the rules of the Government's Entertainment Tax.

WHITECROSS STREET, looking towards St James' Square. The two buildings at the back of the Square were the Hospital and Dispensary, opened in 1868. The original Dispensary had been founded in the town in 1810. There was, at first, the capacity for six in-patients in the new hospital.

BELOW: UNVEILING MONMOUTH WAR MEMORIAL, St James' Square, 6 October 1921. Ex-soldiers J. Jenkins and J. Pembridge sound 'The Last Post' following the unveiling performed by Major Reade DSO MC, headmaster of Monmouth Boys' School (see page 73). Among those present on the platform with him were the Mayor, A.T. Blake; Canon Harding; Revd A.E. Monahan (Vicar of Monmouth); and Major A.C. Tweedy (town clerk). The harmonium was played by G.T. Bennett.

ST JAMES' SQUARE, C. 1925, or perhaps even sooner after the unveiling of the war memorial. Manns' Garage moved to its present site in Whitecross Street in the late 1930s.

CARTREF, ST JAMES' SQUARE, C. 1905. The Hospital moved from Cartref to the new building on the Hereford Road in 1903. In 1907, the 'French Sisters' were running a private school in the building, offering boarders and day pupils lessons in French, music, painting, drawing, needlework and general education. Soon after, a children's home was established there, a use which continues today.

WYEBRIDGE LANE, C. 1904. The occasion has not yet been identified. The reverse of the postcard is date-stamped July 1905. On the extreme right is Mrs Morgan, who acted as a midwife. The woman near her in white with a flat-iron is Mrs Davies. Part of the heavily populated riverside area, between St James' Street and the quayside, the street was renowned for the effort its inhabitants put into street decoration on every suitable occasion.

BELOW: THE SAME STREET, also known as Granville Street, during peace celebrations in 1919. The banner reads: 'We are children of Heroes. We thank God for bringing them safely home'.

MATHEW AND SARAH ANNE PEARCE, with, perhaps, four of their twenty-one children at No. 6, Upper Wyeside. In 1881, their children numbered two, so it may be reasonable to date the photograph to around 1890. He was an oil merchant, rag-and-bone dealer and boat owner. In addition the family ran the common lodging house, 'Pearce's Model', seen on the left.

SWIFT'S COURT, off Granville Street, one of the high density 'courts' demolished in the slum clearances of the 1930s.

MONMOUTH AND THE RIVER WYE, c. 1870, looking downstream towards Wye Bridge, on the left. The quaysides on the far side of the river were called St George's, Little and Hyam's Quays. It is not clear whether the trows in the foreground are loading or unloading stone. Note the long towing-rope running towards the bottom of the photograph, used by the bow-hauliers to manhandle the barges along the river.

TOP, RIGHT: THE QUAYSIDE BELOW WYE BRIDGE, c. 1865. Although badly faded, the photograph shows the bridge before it was widened in 1879, and the quayside before the school was extended in the 1890s.

RIGHT: T. FULLER'S BOATHOUSE AND LANDING, c. 1880. The public landing steps are now here, part of the old quayside upstream from Wye Bridge. The canoe was probably hired from Fuller, who was based at the Waterman's Arms (see over).

WYE BRIDGE AND THE END OF WYEBRIDGE STREET, two views of the same position showing the changes made in the 1890s with the demolition of the Waterman's Arms for the extension of Monmouth School. The bottom photograph was taken in around 1905. The buildings in the centre of the picture were demolished for the construction of the A40 in the early 1960s.

ABOVE: WYEBRIDGE STREET from the bridge, 1885. The decorations were erected by Mr Fuller of the Waterman's Arms (left) for the Monmouthshire Show. The hanging canoe with the motto 'Paddle Your Own Canoe' reflects Fuller's business of hiring out boats of all kinds for public use on the river.

BELOW: WEYBRIDGE STREET, c. 1905, with the school gates on the left. The names of the workmen are not known.

WYE BRIDGE, Monday 29 October 1900. The arrival of the Duke and Duchess of York for their visit to the Hendre, home of Lord and Lady Llangattock. The future King George V and Queen Mary had arrived at May Hill station and were then led in procession to Agincourt Square (see page 86). The house on the left was demolished to make way for the A40 bypass in the early 1960s.

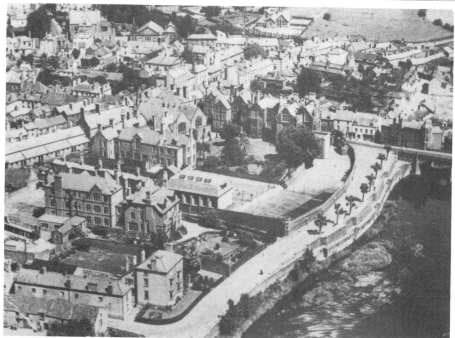

MONMOUTH SCHOOL AND RIVERSIDE, C. 1930. Weirhead Street is bottom left, Wye Bridge is centre right.

CRUTWELL'S ISLAND, downstream from Wye Bridge, with access from the east bank, by the school playing field. The gardens were laid out through the efforts of R.W. Crutwell, a master at Monmouth school, as a memorial to Cecil Hugh Sutherland, school cricket captain, who drowned in the Wye in March 1921.

MAY HILL, LOOKING ALONG THE STAUNTON ROAD from the Monmouth direction, c. 1890. The reason for the decorations has not yet been established. All the buildings shown, except the one on the right, have now gone including the turnpike house, the porch of which is by the left standard of the decorative arch. At the end of the railings on the left was the access to the gasworks. The Hadnock Road turning was beyond the buildings on the left.

ABOVE, RIGHT: MAY HILL STATION UNDER FLOOD, probably 1910. The Wye runs across the middle of the picture; the gable ends of the Quayside buildings can be seen middle, left. The Ross to Monmouth railway line was opened in 1873, Monmouth's second rail link with the outside world. The continuation to Monmouth Troy Station and the Pontypool line (and, from 1876, the Wye Valley line to Chepstow) was opened in 1874 after the construction of the bridge over the Wye (see page 120). The Ross line was closed in 1959.

RIGHT: TENNIS CLUB, c. 1925, May Hill. Standing left to right: ? Fussell, Marjorie Page, Bert Cossens, -?-, Joe Chivers, Gwyneth Howell, Hilda Bricknell, -?-, Phyllis Morris, D. Smith (boy), -?-, Dai Jones, -?-, ? Biddle, Florrie Hill. Front row: Marjorie?, ? Farmer, Howard Bowen, ? Breakwell, Arthur Smith, -?-, ? Breakwell.

CHARLES ROLLS AND HIS BALLOON, Monmouth Gasworks, 1906. Rolls is in the basket on the right. His father, Lord Llangattock, is standing next but one to the right. Lady Llangattock is to the left of the basket. Easter ballooning meets occurred almost annually in Monmouth until Rolls' death in 1910.

LEFT: AN EARLIER MEETING, c. 1900. Town gas was used for inflation, hence the need to launch from May Hill, close to the gasworks. The balloon in the photograph is obscuring May Hill station. The gasworks is in the foreground, right, Staunton Road is on the left.

TOP, LEFT: THE GASWORKS AND THE TIMBER YARD of the sawmills, May Hill, with the town in the background.

THE NAVAL TEMPLE, THE KYMIN, 21 October 1905. Monmouth's celebrations for the centenary of the Battle of Trafalgar and death of Nelson were presided over by Lady Llangattock, one of the foremost collectors of Nelson memorabilia of the period. She is seen here standing between the two central flagpoles with Lord Llangattock and the Mayor of Monmouth, G.R. Edwards. The events on the Kymin culminated in the formation of the word 'Nelson' by the assembled schoolchildren drawn up in ranks. The Naval Temple, visited by Nelson during his short stay in Monmouth in 1802, was restored in 1882, when the sloping-roofed rustic canopy was added. This has now been removed.

BOY SCOUTS ON THE KYMIN, 1918. The scoutmaster, William Walters (back row, centre), was a monumental-mason, with his yard at Dixton Gate. His niece, Alice Rogers, née Wood, who has helped to name some of those present, is standing on the left of the rear group, in white. Front row, left to right: Leslie Pepperdine, -?-, -?-, Ken Howell, Ron Monnington, Fred Wood, -?-, Leslie Rendle, -?-. Back row: to the right of the scoutmaster, Len Cook, Leslie Hayward, -?-, Len Walters, -?-, -?-.

JOHN ARTHUR 'HOKEY-POKEY' EVANS, c. 1930, with his dog, 'Nana', climbing to his cottage on the Kymin. Born in 1854, he is remembered locally as a solitary, bearded old man, living in a run-down cottage with his dog and his chickens. In his early life he trained as an artist, and there are many examples of his work in Monmouth, including a large collection in the museum. He earned his nickname from his ownership of a small confectionary shop from which he claimed to be the first in Monmouth to sell an ice-cream called 'hokey-pokey'. He was devastated by the death of his wife and lived out the latter half of his existence in a gradual decline until his death in 1936.

LEFT AND ABOVE: MONMOUTH SCHOOL AND THE QUEEN'S HEAD INN from Almshouse Street. Top, left shows the school as rebuilt during the 1860s and, below, the further alterations made towards the end of the century. The Queen's Head has undergone many face-changes since it was built in the sixteenth century. The original stone and timber have been plastered over and clad with stone; the profile has been changed by the addition and removal of gables; and latterly mock 'black-and-white' work has been added (photographed above in 1924).

MONMOUTH SCHOOL, an undated photograph of a Classics lesson in progress, from a school prospectus.

ABOVE: REMNANTS OF COTTAGES, WIERHEAD STREET, c. 1950. The view is across the dog-leg corner of Glendower Street/Almshouse Street, from the end of Worcester Street. Wierhead Street ran down to the Wye quayside and, at one time, it contained the workhouse before the new building was opened on the Hereford Road in 1868. The Monmouth School hall now stands on the site of the cottages.

LEFT: THE JONES' ALMSHOUSES, ALMSHOUSE STREET, c. 1860. Re-built in 1842, the houses were in use as dwellings until the new Almshouses were built by the Haberdashers off Whitecross Street in 1961.

A.W. FERNEYHOUGH'S SHOP, St Mary Street, 1910. The proprietor is on the right, with his wife, Gertrude, son Reginald (in the hat), Charles Wigmore (foreman baker), and Leonard Powell. Mr Wigmore took over the business in the early 1920s when Mr Ferneyhough moved to Church Street as a grocer. Reg Ferneyhough continued the business as a sweet shop until recently.

HOWELL'S BUTCHERS, St Mary Street, c. 1895. Mr Howell may be seen with his butcher's tray on his shoulder.

THE CORNER OF ALMSHOUSE STREET AND ST MARY STREET, c. 1950. The building on the corner was originally a malthouse, part of Cossens' brewery. It is now used by Monmouth School.

MONMOUTH FIRE BRIGADE, 1929, in Whitecross Street. A new engine and pump had just been delivered. The fire station was in Whitecross Street at this time, before a combined fire and ambulance station was opened in St Mary Street. The driver in the picture was J. Payne, with Capt. W. Biddle, fire chief, next to him.

ABOVE, LEFT: ST MARY'S CHURCH, before 1881, when the rebuilding of the Georgian church began. The opportunity was also taken to tidy up the churchyard, no longer in active use since the opening of the cemetery in 1851.

LEFT: THE OPENING OF THE WINTER ASSIZES, 6 February 1936. The procession is heading along Whitecross Street for a service in St Mary's. Lord Chief Justice Lord Hewart is at the rear, with the mayor, Revd Owen-Jones and the town clerk, Maj. A.C. Tweedy, in the centre. The criminal cases were dealt with on the same day in less than an hour. A GWR platelayer from near Abergavenny, who had attacked his wife and daughter with an axe, was sentenced to 15 months hard labour and a colliery labourer from Abersychan was bound over for stealing a pony.

LEFT: ST MARY'S CHURCH SPIRE, July 1864. 'On Saturday last the topstone of the steeple was duly set, and the weathercock, newly gilded, was restored to its former elevation. The contractor hoisted some gay flags on the summit of the tower in honour of the event.' (*Beacon*, 23 July 1864.) Earlier in May one of the workmen had fallen while descending the scaffold. He was not badly hurt, but when it was discovered that his fall had been caused by a recurrence of fainting fits, his services were 'judiciously dispensed with'. The contractor was Henry Hughes of Bristol and 50 ft of the spire were rebuilt.

ABOVE: THE WEATHERCOCK, St Mary's Church, 1884. The cock was regilded at the workshops of Mr T.M. Preece, coachbuilder, Church Street (seen here crouching). Champney Powell, the mayor, is third from the left. Miss Rosa Powell paid for the work.

AGINCOURT SQUARE, looking into Priory Street, August 1914. Jarrett, the stationer and bookseller, on the left, has newspaper placards outside about the Battle of Mons and Sir John French. W.E. Day, ironmonger, moved soon afterwards to the premises on the far side of Castle Hill, occupied by Symonds and Cooper, drapers, in the photograph. Day's old premises became the Carlton Cafe.

MONMOUTH PAGEANT, 1911, looking along Priory Street with Castle Hill on the left.

ABOVE: W.E. DAY, NO. 24, AGINCOURT SQUARE, c. 1920. The premises became Woolworth's in the mid-1930s and were subsequently demolished and rebuilt.

RIGHT: CASTLE HILL, pre-1915, with the band of the RMRE(M). The occasion has yet to be identified.

COLONEL JOHN FRANCIS VAUGHAN with officers of the Royal Monmouthshire Militia at Monmouth Castle, 1860. Colonel Vaughan (in the centre of the photograph, hand on hip) had joined the Militia as a Captain in 1836. He became Honorary Colonel in 1858 and retired in 1877. In the background is Great Castle House (1673), in one of the few pictures to show it without the later single-storey extensions on each side. The Militia Mess was established in Great Castle House in 1878.

MONMOUTH JUNIOR IMPERIAL LEAGUE, Christmas fancy dress party, 1937, in Castle Hill House. The League, the Monmouth Branch of which was formed in 1925, was the forerunner of the Young Conservatives. The group can be broken down into four rows for naming purposes. Front row, left to right: Cyril Call; his wife; Beryl Wigmore; Frank Morris; Doreen Dobbs; Irene French; Iris Williams; Ada Bevington; Pat Arnold; Joan Alsop. Second row: mostly un-identified though the policeman is Henry Spencer; Gladys Moore is behind his left shoulder; the gypsy girl is Dorothy Jones and at the end of the row in glasses is Ken Howell. Third row: fourth from left – Claud Gouldsmith; fifth – Ray Lewis; ninth – Frank Hoddel; eleventh – John Young; twelfth – Victoria Watkins; fourteenth – 'Granny' Hunt (who acted as chaperone on such occasions); thirteenth, end of row – Doris Jones. Back row: above the vicar – Len Hunt; Hitler – Eric Willis; with paper crown – Ruby French; the next three women – Eileen Wilson, Vi Roach, Neta French; with bowler hat – Don Howes; end of row – ? Morgan.

THE NELSON MUSEUM, Glendower Street, opened on 16 April 1924, in the gymnasium given to the town by Lord Llangattock (see page 82/33). When Lady Llangattock bequeathed her Nelson collection to the town, she had envisaged it being housed in the Rolls Hall. It was nevertheless decided that the ailing gymnasium would make an ideal museum. Opened by Lady Shelley-Rolls, the last surviving child of the Llangattocks, the museum was transferred to Priory Street in 1969.

THE NEW MARKET HALL, (left) Priory Street, 1963. The fire destroyed the premises of the *Monmouthshire Beacon* which had been resident since 1876. The salvaged building, minus clock tower and superstructure, was re-opened as the Nelson Museum and Local History Centre in 1969.

MONMOUTH POSTMEN, at the rear of the post office in Priory Street, c. 1920. Left to right: Davies (clerk, PO); Kear; -?-; Savory; -?-; -?-; Marr (postmaster); Freeman; Charles; Llywarch; Preece; -?-; Sysum; Dobbs; George Jenkins; Savory; ? Powell; ? Freeman; Mapp. George Jenkins retired from the Post Office in 1933 and died aged 88 in 1959. He served with the South Wales Borderers from 1890 to 1897, spending four years overseas in Egypt and Gibraltar. He produced the wool and silk thread picture mount reproduced here during that time. The photograph in the centre shows him with his wife and the first of his two daughters. In 1900 he was called from the Army Reserve to fight with his former regiment in South Africa. The diaries he kept during the two years of active service against the Boers are now in Monmouth Museum.

MONMOUTH SLAUGHTERHOUSES, August 1902, during preparations for the Coronation ox-roasting. The slaughterhouses were built in the mid-1830s as a means of supporting the new Priory Street and Market Hall. On the right of the photograph, with hand in pocket, is J. Mackie. On the opposite side, in the straw-boater, is G.P. Tippins jnr. To his right is C.N. Ballinger, to his left F. Howell (see page 57). Standing with his hand on the victim is W. Peachey.

TOP, RIGHT: OX-ROASTING, 9 August 1902, Monmouth Cattle Market. Mr J. Mackie, with ladle, was in charge of the spit and later assisted with the carving of the beast, which was distributed by ticket to the poor of the town.

RIGHT: OX-ROASTING COMMITTEE, Silver Jubilee Celebrations, 1935. On the steps, back row, left to right: R. Mackie, J. Mackie, J. Bullock, W. Biddle. Second row: H. Shilbach, D. Smith, W. Lambert. Front row: T. Little (boy), H. Watson, C. Hancocks, C. Jones (mayor), A. Williams, J. Little (boy in front). Standing with the ox, from the left: W. Hunt, T. Little, W. Howells, J. Little, T. Hutton, E. Probyn. Note the worn stones of the parapet on the right of the picture, used by generations of butchers to sharpen knives.

MONMOUTH HOUSE, PRIORY STREET, C. 1900. The Temperance Hotel, the sign of which can just be seen on the left, was opened in 1895. Hughes the outfitters was opened in around 1884. The premises are currently occupied by Mervyn Fellows, menswear, and Wilkes, florists.

RIGHT: W.A. CALL had his business as a photographic publisher further along the street at No. 3. An accomplished musician, he is best remembered as a photographer and puppeteer. Many of the photographs in the museum collections were taken by Call, some being salvaged from his studio after his death in 1964. He was a skilful architectural photographer, but also produced hundreds of landscape views in postcard form or larger which he sold from his shop – 'The County Studio'. His marionette shows were professionally staged and he regularly performed at Blackpool during the holiday season. He is seen here with 'Dorothea', a rather 'fast' female, reputedly based on a Monmouth original. The other puppet is 'Cuthbert' and below is the stage, with 'Dorothea' in the centre.

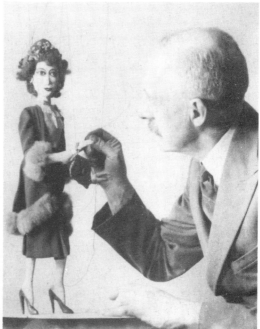

TOP, LEFT: MONMOUTH PRIORY, C. 1875. The use of the Priory buildings as a school began in the late-eighteenth century, when a retired naval officer ran a private school for boys. By 1804, it had become a charity school, which developed into the Monmouth National School in 1814. In 1896 the girls were transferred to Overmonnow and the premises were enlarged, with an extension on the churchyard side. Priory Street Boys' School continued until 1972. The Premises became a youth hostel in 1978.

LEFT: MONMOUTH BOYS' SCHOOL, SCHOLARSHIP BOYS, 1913. Back row, left to right: C. Bricknall; T. Farmer; C. Gobey; H. Hunt; H. Cumbley; D. Edwards; L. Cook. Front row: A. Giles; T. Mayfield; Mr A. Reade (headmaster); Mr A. Weightman; F. Larey; J.C.R. Price.

ABOVE: PRIORY STREET SCHOOL, 1918. In September 1914, the headmaster of the school, Arthur Reade, enlisted in the army, returning at the end of the war as a Major with the MC and the DSO. The photograph shows the party given in the school to welcome him home.

MONNOW MILL AND THE RIVER MONNOW, C. 1880, with St Mary's Church and Great Castle House in the background. The weir and the mill leet can be seen in the foreground.

THE RACECOURSE, Vauxhall, C. 1925, seen from Monmouth Castle. The grandstands can be seen in the distance. Racing continued here until the mid-1930s. This is the only photograph in the museum collection to show racing in progress.

A ROYAL AIRCRAFT FACTORY BE2 AEROPLANE ON VAUXHALL, 25 August 1912, the first aeroplane to land in Monmouth. Lieutenants Fox and Ashton had flown the plane from Lark Hill, on Salisbury Plain, via Weymouth. They were prevented from leaving by flooding on Vauxhall, Lieutenant Fox eventually flying off alone because of the boggy ground.

MONMOUTH MUNICIPAL ELECTRICITY GENERATING WORKS, Osbaston, c. 1920, with Madge Windsor, daughter of the manager. The works were opened in 1899, built on the remains of Monmouth Forge.

CHURCH STREET FROM AGINCOURT SQUARE, c. 1900. Key's chemist's shop had changed hands by 1902 and J.H. Grant, tobacconist, moved from No. 3 Agincourt Square to No. 18 after 1906. Note the butcher's shop in Church Street, a reminder of the medieval use of the street as the shambles for the town: the street was at one time called Butchers' Row. The Punch House, on the right, was given the name in 1896, being called The Wine Vaults before then.

VETERAN'S RUGBY MATCH, 31 March 1921. Back row, left to right: F. Probyn; J. Daniels; H.W. Rowland; R. Hughes; V. Williams. Second row: A.T. Blake (mayor); N.C. Elstob; W. Lewis; J.T. Vizard; T. Hughes; J. Pembridge; L. Merrick; W. Morris; R. Vick; W. Jones; P. Jenkins; C. Fennell; P. Mulcair; F. Park (who dislocated his shoulder); E. Harvey; F. Freeman; G.H. Powell; Major A. Reade; E.T.A. Williams. Third row: H. Russell; A.W. Smith; Douglas Smith; F.H.S. Perkins; W.E. Coldicutt. Front row: W.E. Day; A.C. Morgan; V. Coldicutt; W.J. Morgan (referee); F. Hayward; F. Morris; C.V. Hyam. The match was arranged in aid of Monmouth Hospital (£48 raised), and was followed by dinner at the Beaufort Arms, for which Mr and Mrs Richman created a decorated table in the form of a rugby pitch, with the players represented by soda water bottles (below).

CHURCH STREET, c. 1920. The three shops, Wilde (jeweller), Page (draper), and the Monmouth Cycle Co. were at Nos. 3, 5, and 7 Church Street, respectively, in 1920. By 1926, Wilde had moved to No. 14 Church Street. No. 3 is currently Brian Stevens' bookshop, No. 5 the National Trust shop and No. 7 Steeples restaurant.

THE BEAUFORT ARMS TAP, C. 1870. Now demolished, this was part of the Beaufort Arms Hotel. It was used by the grooms, ostlers and servants of the hotel guests. The Bull Inn in Agincourt Square is to the left, the Beaufort to the right.

THE SHIRE HALL, Agincourt Square, c. 1897. The date has been assumed from the vestiges of decoration on the front of the King's Head Hotel (right) which may relate to the celebration of Queen Victoria's Diamond Jubilee. The railings between the arches of the Shire Hall were removed during the Second World War. The large stone urns on the parapet were taken down when it was repaired in the 1960s. It has been suggested recently that if the urns can be found, they should be replaced. The coach, from the Beaufort Arms Hotel, would have been used to convey guests to and from the railway stations.

THE UNVEILING OF THE ROLLS MEMORIAL, Agincourt Square, 19 October 1911. Charles Rolls' father, Lord Llangattock, is speaking, with the Mayor of Monmouth, W. Sambrook, on his right. The unveiling was performed by Lord Raglan, who is sitting at the end of the first row on the right. Sir Goscombe John RA, who modelled the statue, was present but has not yet been identified. The *Beacon* reported that Lord Llangattock, in the course of his speech, was 'greatly affected and was at times almost completely overcome'. (See page 118.)

ABOVE AND OPPOSITE: COMING OF AGE CELEBRATIONS, John Maclean Rolls, 1891. The roasting of an ox in Agincourt Square on Thursday 30 April 1891 was part of a day of festivities which were the culmination of several days of celebration marking the twenty-first birthday of the heir to the Hendre estate. A dinner for the tenants of the estate was the opening event on the previous Saturday, the actual birthday, when over 500 were entertained in the covered tennis court at the Hendre. Thursday's events began with the lighting of the fires in the huge double brick fireplaces built in Agincourt Square for the ox-roast, under the supervision of Mr C. Morgan and Mr E. James. While the ox roasted (it was ready at 8 p.m.) J.M. Rolls, with members of his family and friends, was met at Drybridge by the Mayor and Corporation, the Fire Brigade, local Friendly Societies (their banners can be seen in the photographs) and the band of the RMEM, and led in procession through the town. In Agincourt Square, a short

pause enabled schoolchildren to sing 'Many Happy Returns of the Day', followed by a verse of the National Anthem from all the crowd. The procession continued through the streets, arriving eventually in Glendower Street at the site of the new gymnasium which John Allan Rolls, J.M.'s father, was having built as a gift to the town (see page 66). Here, John Mclean laid the foundation stone of the new building, before continuing in procession to the Rolls Hall, an earlier gift (see page 28/29), for an organ recital and presentations from the Primrose League. Tea and cake were provided for local children in their schools at 3.30 p.m., paid for from the subscriptions raised by the committee set up to organize the town celebrations. Mr T. Farror of Church Street was the contractor for the children's tea, having submitted the lowest tender, at 5d. per head. The day was rounded-off with rustic sports and a grand torchlight procession.

ABOVE: PEACE CELEBRATIONS, Agincourt Square, 18 July 1919. A committee chaired by the mayor, G.R. Edwards, organized two days of celebrations to mark the end of the war, beginning with a march of the demobilized from Troy station to dinner in the Rolls Hall. In Agincourt Square they were met by the mayor, and paused for a photograph before continuing to the Rolls Hall for dinner (see page 34).

TOP, LEFT: AGINCOURT SQUARE, 1918/19. The occasion has yet to be identified, although it has a military flavour, and the mayor presiding is G.R. Edwards. In December 1918 captured German field guns were received in the town, and this may be the subject of the photograph. Notice the steam wagon to the left of the picture.

LEFT: AGINCOURT SQUARE, 1914, apparently taken on the same day as the view on page 62. The shop premises on the left are now Barclays Bank, Victoria Wine, the vacant former W.H. Smith, and Ruby Tuesday. Then they were: Gilbey, wine merchant; Lane, tobacconist; Griffiths, jeweller; Yearsley, hairdresser and tabacconist; Bowers, sweets; Jarrett, stationer.

ABOVE: THE VISIT OF THE DUKE AND DUCHESS OF YORK, 29 October 1900, showing their arrival in Agincourt Square. The visit was a private one, to stay with the Llangattocks at the Hendre. Because of this, the official welcome in the Shire Hall was extremely brief, with the mayor handing the address of welcome to the Duke, who handed back a written reply. The Royal party then retired to the Hendre for a visit rendered even more subdued by the fact that the Royal couple were in mourning for Prince Christian Victor. Most of the planned excursions were cancelled, although a trip to Tintern in Charles Rolls' 12 hp Panhard car was managed. The Duke consoled himself with four days of shooting, during which 3,500 pheasant, wild duck, hares and rabbits were killed.

RIGHT: AGINCOURT SQUARE, 1953, during and after the parade of the Royal Monmouthshire Royal Engineers to mark their receipt of the Freedom of the Borough of Monmouth.

AGINCOURT SQUARE, 1897, during the ox-roast to celebrate Queen Victoria's Diamond Jubilee.

KING'S HEAD HOTEL, C. 1900, possibly showing Dr Rutherford Harris of Llangibby Castle electioneering on the way to a short-lived victory in the Parliamentary election of that year. He was unseated on petition by his opponent for slander.

CORONATION CHURCH PARADE, Agincourt Square, 22 June 1911, leaving the Shire Hall *en route* for St Mary's. Other events during the day included a pageant organized by Mr Reade of the Priory Street Boys' School, sports and a torchlight procession. Note the original premises of W.H. Smith on the left, currently the Agincourt Optical Centre.

AGINCOURT SQUARE, *c.* 1950, with Mr Cecil Mackie leading the sheep, on the way to the Priory Street slaughterhouses, and Mr Bert James, who worked for Lewis, butcher, of No. 76 Monnow Street, bringing up the rear.

NO. 1, AGINCOURT SQUARE, 1919. The exact date and occasion have yet to be fixed, but the photograph probably records the opening of a YMCA room in these premises. The wreath above the door carries the message: 'In Memory of Our Fallen Comrades'.

NO. 19 AGINCOURT SQUARE, c. 1885. The Militia soldiers were lodging there. In 1890, the Quartermaster of the RME Militia was inviting applications from anyone able to offer lodgings, at the rate of fourpence per night for each bed actually occupied. Also in 1890, the Editor of the *Beacon*, writing in anticipation of the annual training which brought the Militia to the town, acknowledged the economic importance to the town of the influx of money, commenting that the disadvantages associated with the visitation (rowdy and drunken behaviour) had decreased over recent years. The premises are currently Victoria Wine.

TOP, LEFT: THE TOP OF MONNOW STREET FROM AGINCOURT SQUARE, before the street was widened in 1883/4. The decorations probably relate to the wedding of Lady Blanche Somerset in 1883. The widening was effected by demolishing the protruding shops on the left and re-building in line with the shop on the extreme left (No. 6 Monnow Street, currently Jetsaver Travel). Opposite, beneath the flag, is No. 3, now French the baker.

LEFT: MONNOW STREET FROM AGINCOURT SQUARE, c. 1890. The premises of William Hall & Co. (No. 1 Monnow Street) are currently occupied by Boots the Chemist. The two entrance pillars survive.

ABOVE: THE TOP OF MONNOW STREET, looking towards Agincourt Square, c. 1900. The street widening, completed in 1884, provided premises for Kennington Hall, outfitters, Nos. 8 and 10 Monnow Street, seen here on the right. A commemorative plaque on the corner of the building records the widening, with the initials of the then mayor, G.P. Tippins. When details of the proposed plaque were first revealed at a Council meeting, several councillors objected because they had not been consulted. One suggested sarcastically that a marble bust of the mayor might be more appropriate. The street is probably decorated for the visit of the Duke and Duchess of York.

ABOVE: MONNOW STREET, March 1947. Mr W. Biddle, Borough Surveyor and Sanitary Inspector, left, issuing dried milk for distribution. Next to him is Gwen Bundy and, next to her, Fred Herbert of the Cafe Royal. In the background, beneath the 'Wye Valley' sign is Percy Macey, manager of the Red and White bus company who, at this time, was having to arrange for his buses to be parked at the Castle because of flooding in the bus station garage. On the right of the picture is Howard Bowen. The names of the men with the boat are not known.

LEFT: MONNOW STREET, March 1947. A heavy blizzard on Saturday 15 March (top), was followed by a gale and heavy rain. By Wednesday large areas of the town were under water (below).

MONNOW STREET, C. 1895. On the left is the Worcester Lodge pub, now an Italian restaurant.

NO. 70 MONNOW STREET, March 1947. Mr Wilding and his son taking delivery of emergency supplies from Mr J. Preece, with Mr Lock providing support (see page 94).

ABOVE AND OPPOSITE: MONNOW STREET, c. 1890s. No firm date has been established, and the reason for the decorations can only be surmized. The Silver Wedding of Lord and Lady Llangattock in 1893 is a possibility, or perhaps John Allan Rolls' elevation to the peerage as Lord Llangattock in 1892. Tar was sprayed on Monnow Street in 1912, apparently the first attempt to provide a more permanent surface than the packed dirt shown here, which was usually either dusty or muddy. In the photograph on the right a paved pedestrian crossing can be seen. On the right of the left-hand photograph is G.R. Edwards' furniture shop, (currently Agincourt fashions). Further up the street are the Butchers' Arms (Burton's), and R. Walker, ironmonger (also Burton's). On the other side of the street is the Vine Tree Inn, with the King's Arms just before the second flag (later demolished for Peacock's, now itself under development).

MONNOW STREET, two views from roughly the same viewpoint, the top, *c.* 1885, below, *c.* 1908. The premises on the right of the top photograph are currently occupied by Dorothy Perkins, those on the left by W.H. Smith Travel.

CHILDREN'S PAGEANT, Monnow Street, 8 June 1908, with the May Queen leading (see page 20). On the right of the photograph is No. 38 Monnow Street (see page 102). Note the collecting box on a pole to reach contributions from first-floor windows.

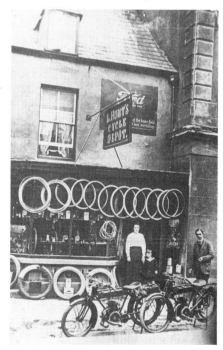

NO. 101, MONNOW STREET, c. 1930. Hunt's later moved (c. 1937) across the street to the present garage premises. The building on the right was demolished soon after 1946 to make an entry into the new bus station. No. 101 is currently Marlene's Cafe.

NO. 38 MONNOW STREET, C. 1880. 'George Higgins, Grocer and Tea Dealer' (see page 114). Note the boy with the yoke to carry whatever his two companions are sitting on, perhaps paraffin containers. The premises are currently occupied by Dixons.

HOWARD BOWEN, in his grocery shop, No. 78 Monnow Street. The business closed in January 1979. Mr Bowen served on the Borough Council for 42 years, becoming Mayor of Monmouth eight times. He was made an Alderman in 1945 and, in 1970, he and his wife received the Freedom of the Borough. He died in 1983.

MONNOW STREET, 1914, with Jack and Mabel Smith (brother and sister) standing in the doorway of their shop (behind the man with bike). The premises later became Partridge the bakers and are currently Peacock's.

NO. 27, MONNOW STREET, Nailors Lane on the right. Baynham Bros. seem to have changed into just Hubert Baynham between 1914 and 1920. By the 1930s, the shop had become McEwan and Baynham, and included sports goods among the stock.

A TRACTION ENGINE ACCIDENT, Monnow Street, 19 April 1912. The engine had fallen through the weighbridge situated in the street while on the way from Devon to Llandenny with three van loads of furniture. The driver, Charles Charles, and the steerer, John Wilkinson, both from Weston-super-Mare, were unhurt. The engine was raised with the help of the Council steam-roller and was able to continue the journey.

MONNOW STREET, 1947 flood, looking into the Cattle Market, showing an ingenious alternative to the punts usually deployed in Monmouth's floods.

ACKLAND'S ANGELS, June 1914. Frederick Ackland had drapery shops at No. 54 and No. 93 Monnow Street. The assistants are: back row, left to right: Edith Grindel; Mrs Manns; Mrs Barter. Front row: Miss Robinson; Elsie Downs.

CHIPPENHAM MEAD, C. 1925. The exact date and circumstances have yet to be established.

ABOVE: MONNOW STREET, 1910. In 1914, G. Williams moved down to the next but one building, the Tan House (No. 95) with the oriel window. Between them is No. 93, Ackland's draper (see page 105). On the left of the photograph is the Borough Arms

BELOW: PROBABLY THE SAME 1910 FLOOD as above, looking up Monnow Street from a position outside the cattle market, the Robin Hood Inn on the right.

G.H. WILLIAMS AND FAMILY, c. 1914, at the rear of the Tan House. Left to right: daughter Gertrude, wife Elizabeth, daughter Maude, and her daughter Winifred. George Williams began his business selling bicycles. The garage was continued by his son George Reginald until, in 1946, the premises were sold and became the bus station.

MONNOW BRIDGE, c. 1910. The houses beyond the arch, in Overmonnow, were demolished in 1925, those on the right in the 1930s.

MONNOW GATE, looking up Monnow Street, c. 1910. Built in the late-thirteenth century, the structure is unique in Britain, although such fortified bridges were common to many walled medieval towns sited on rivers. Plans to divert traffic from using the bridge by erecting an alternative crossing over the River Monnow have been put forward several times in the past. Recent damage from passing vehicles, one of them, in 1982, a double-decker bus whose driver forgot he was not in a single-decker, has prompted renewed calls for a ban on traffic, and a new bridge.

THE TANK 'JULIAN' on Monnow Bridge, 5 July 1918. As part of the War Savings campaign, the tank arrived by train at Troy station and was led in procession to Agincourt Square by the Mayor, Corporation and a large crowd headed by Mr J.C. Powell, local hon. secretary of the War Savings Committee. He announced that Monmouth was expected to raise at least £20,000 that day. By 3.45 p.m. over £54,000 had been deposited in the tank, donors being encouraged by a series of speeches, from the mayor, Canon Harding, and Mrs Levett, who reminded the crowd that 'when our soldiers went over the top, they did not count the cost . . .'

DRYBRIDGE HOUSE, 7 August 1906. Field Marshall H.R.H. The Duke of Connaught, General Sir John Maxwell and the Hon. Miles Ponsonby driven by George Webb, during the Duke's visit as Inspector General of the Forces to inspect the RMRE(M). Colonel C.M. Crompton Roberts of Drybridge House acted as host. The party was involved in a car crash near Hay-on-Wye later in the day. No serious damage was done, but the chauffeur of the other car was arrested on suspicion of being drunk, whereupon he threatened to kill himself.

BELOW: GEORGE WEBB at the wheel of his car, with his wife Annie and her sister Sue on the occasion of the latter's wedding, outside his workshop at Croker's Ash, c. 1903. George Webb founded two businesses, the 'Ganarew and West of England Cycle Co.' at Croker's Ash, and the Priory Street Motor Co. in Monmouth, where his 'detachable and divisible rim' for car wheels was made, the forerunner of the spare wheel.

ST THOMAS' SQUARE, September 1888. The cross was erected at the expense of Mr Crompton-Roberts of Drybridge House, using the base of the original cross which is shown standing in the Square in Speed's map of 1611. The photograph shows the first version of the new structure, which was later modified in December 1888, the shaft and head being lengthened and the base steps increased in size (see over). The sculptor was H. Wall of Newport, who also carved the four figures placed in the niches on the head of the cross: St Thomas; St Mary; St Michael and St Cenhadlon.

TOP: ST THOMAS' SQUARE, C. 1865, with the base of the cross in the foreground (see page 111). The strange turret on the church dates from the Arthur Wyatt restoration of 1831, and was replaced in the 1874–80 repair. The houses on the left, which once contained a 'faggot-and-peas' shop, were demolished in 1925.

BELOW: ST THOMAS' SQUARE, C. 1905. The horse trough was installed at the same time as the drinking fountain (left of the church) to commemorate Queen Victoria's Diamond Jubilee in 1897.

TOP: FLOOD, ST THOMAS' SQUARE, c. 1889. On the left is the Green Dragon, and on the right, the Troy House inn.

BELOW: ST THOMAS' SQUARE, c. 1910, looking towards Drybridge Street. In 1889, the Council's surveyor had complained about the congestion and hazard caused by carts left standing around the cross and, no doubt, the installation of the horse trough made things worse.

'ELEPHANT RUNS AMOK. Mop Fair had a lively send off at Monmouth at half past nine on Monday morning. A warm sun shone brightly upon the cheerful scene as farmers pulled in in their carts by the side of the streets and groups of men chatted, in scattered parties, on the weather and market prospects. Suddenly a shrill trumpeting was heard and an elephant was seen to come over Monnow Bridge in the direction of St. Thomas' Square. For a moment, the onlookers gazed on the spectacle with some trepidation, and as the animal did not seem inclined to stop, some began to move nervously away. Another trumpet made the issue complete; with one accord the crowd broke and scattered like magic to various houses and places of safety. The elephant came into St. Thomas' Square and proceeded down Drybridge Street, much to the consternation of women, who pulled their children from the doorsteps into the houses until "jumbo" vanished along the Wonastow Road, while the crowd commenced to congregate once more. Before long the elephant's pursuers overtook him and the animal submitted to being brought back to the Fair with a chain attached to its left leg' (*Beacon*, 9 May 1930). The offending elephant is here shown in the River Monnow, with St Thomas' Church in the background, before its foray into the streets.

LEFT: HIGGINS' GROCERY SHOP, Monnow Bridge, Overmonnow, *c.* 1870. Trade directories record the shop being run by the Higgins family from 1840 to 1937. They also had a shop in Monnow Street (see page 102). The premises are currently used as Overmonnow Post Office.

TOP: CINDERHILL STREET, 1929, looking towards St Thomas' Square. At the left of the photograph is the sweet shop run by Miss Harris and, in the centre, right, the then sub-post office run by Miss Williams.

BOTTOM: LOOKING IN THE OPPOSITE DIRECTION, with the street decorated for the 1935 Jubilee celebrations.

NO. 23, ST THOMAS' SQUARE, 1910, Fred Bevington, (left) having apparently just managed to sell the car shown to the man on the right. Mr Bevington later moved his garage to Monnow Street. The premises shown currently house a launderette and an antiques shop.

TURNPIKE STORES, Cinderhill Street, 1947 flood. The shop, run by Mr Thomas, was famous for home-made ice-cream, a popular Sunday treat, combined with a walk across Chippenham, from where a footbridge crossed the Monnow near the Stores. The building was demolished for the construction of the dual-carriageway of the A40.

TROY STATION, Friday 15 July 1910, during the arrival of the Hon. C.S. Rolls' body. Rolls had been killed when his plane crashed during an aviation meeting in Bournemouth on 12 July. His body had been taken to the family home in London, South Lodge, Rutland Gate, and came from there to Monmouth for burial in Llangattock churchyard on 16 July. The vicars of Monmouth (Revd C.F. Reeks) and Overmonnow (Revd F. Dudley) can just be seen in the top photograph leading the coffin off the platform.

TROY STATION, c. 1900. Mr R. Gooding was stationmaster at that time, and he is perhaps standing on the right of the group in the photograph. None of the others have been identified. The station was opened in 1857 with the arrival of the line from Pontypool,

Monmouth's first railway link. The footbridge shown in the photograph was erected in 1894, two years after a Coroner's jury had strongly recommended the Great Western Railway to provide a bridge following the death of a man crossing the line. The bridge was built by Finch & Co. of Chepstow. RIGHT: THE REFRESHMENT ROOM at Troy station was established in 1886, and continued to operate for a time after the station closed to passengers in 1959. The photograph, taken in September 1959, is of Mrs N. Wallett who served in the refreshment room.

WYE BRIDGE, ROSS AND MONMOUTH RAILWAY, 1873. '... a preliminary trial of strength of the last bridge over the Wye, at the Gamblings, which unites the railway to the Great Western system, was made on Sunday afternoon, and was eminently successful. A train, consisting of engine, tender, car and 22 wagons laden with ballast, and in which were also 60 men – a weight of 200 tons – was conducted over the bridge.... There was a large number of persons present, and the ballast trucks having been unloaded on the Wyesham side, these were speedily occupied by living beings anxious to have the first trip over the last span of line. The bridge is of lattice form, and has been constructed by Messrs. Finch and Co. of Chepstow, the contractors for the other bridges on the line. The bridge has been erected under the superintendence of Mr Bailiff, foreman of the company, and it is gratifying to note that no accident of any kind has had to be recorded during the time it was in hand.' (*Beacon*, 13 December 1873). The link from May Hill to Troy Station was opened on 1 May 1874.

THE RAILWAY VIADUCT, Monmouth, c. 1910. The fisherman is James Edwards, a carpenter, brother of Mrs Gertrude Ferneyhough (see page 56). The viaduct was opened on 1 July 1861, extending the Pontypool–Monmouth line across the Wye to Wyesham exchange. From Troy station the line is carried on a series of stone arches, which consumed 9,000 yards of masonry and 3,000 yards of concrete in building. During the construction of the girder bridge across the river, in May 1859, the *Beacon* reported on a 'nuisance' which it hoped would cease before an accident happened: 'To cross the girders is a feat greatly desired by the multitude. ... Some of the unwashed from Wyebridge Lane have taken advantage of the popular fancy and have posted themselves on the bridge, stating that they are authorized to take a toll, ... the sum demanded varying from a copper to sixpence, according to the dress and position of the gulled ones.'

MR A. WILLIAMS, builder, (second from the left, standing) with workers during the construction of an unidentified building, possibly the electricity works at Osbaston. The men sitting on the scaffolding are, left, Mr Cambley, right, Mr Leddington.

GEORGE 'CORBETT' PEMBRIDGE, who in 1911 aged 21, defeated Johnnie Matheson, 'the Fighting Scot', at the National Sporting Club. In July of the same year he knocked out Charlie Price of Newport during an 'Assault-at-Arms' in the gymnasium, Monmouth.

MONMOUTH'S FIRST VAD UNIT of the First World War, photographed at the rear of St James' House. The Voluntary Aid Detachments of volunteers from the British Red Cross Society, the St John Ambulance Brigade and the Territorial Force Association were intended to fill gaps in the Army Medical Services on the Home Front. Back row, left to right: Watkins; Simmons; Jarret; Simmons; Nicholls; Wiseman; -?-; Preece; -?-; -?-; Coussins. Middle row: Richards; Barrow; Evans; Harding; Williams; Woodhouse; Griffin; Vizard; Barrie. Front row: Lowe; Blake; Harding; Wiseman.

GILBERT AND ARTHUR JONES, c. 1910. Their parents ran Taylor & Jones, the Ironmongers in Monnow Street.

THE MAYOR OF MONMOUTH, 1933/34, Cllr. Bruton, at an unidentified event in the foyer of the cinema, Church Street. To his right are Mrs Blake and Mrs O. Jones, and Alderman A.T. Blake is on the right of the picture. Other members of the Council are in the background.

RED AND WHITE BUS CREW, Monmouth, March 1941. Standing, left to right: Lill Blythe; Tom Hearne; Nancy Butler; Francis (Bill) Hodgson; Beryl Williams; Jack Handly. Behind, left to right: Freddie Herbert; Nell Gleed; Dennis Cornwell. At the time the buses were used to ferry munitions workers to Caerwent.

THE MAYOR AND CORPORATION OF MONMOUTH, 1907/8, at the rear of the Shire Hall (Beaufort Arms Court). Standing, left to right: Macebearer; F.C. Williams; H.F. Perkins; W. Sambrook; A.T. Blake; C.N. Ballinger; J.H. Grant; T.H. Jones; Macebearer. Sitting, left to right: H.T. Baillie; G.R. Edwards; A.E. Jones (deputy mayor); Hon. J.M. Rolls (mayor); B.H. Deakin (town clerk); Alderman G.P. Tippins; K. Hall.

CARNIVAL AND FÊTE, 25 June 1931. The decorated Fiat car of Dorothy Evans (driving, with Nini Call, front, and Muriel Farthing) in Chippenhamgate Street, preparing for the Carnival procession. The event raised £300 for the Hospital Fund.

WYASTONE LEYS AND THE LITTLE DOWARD, c. 1910. The Leys had been built in 1795 and was enlarged, and renamed, when it was acquired by the Bannerman family in 1861/2. Earlier in the century, the house had belonged to Richard Blakemore, a local industrialist, who erected an iron observation tower on the summit of the Little Doward hill, shown here. It was dismantled in 1920. Also shown in the photograph above is Chapel Farm. The original road from Monmouth to Ross ran along the riverside past the farm, climbing steeply over the valley side at Ganarew. A new road, on the line of the present A40, was made in 1820.

MEMBERS OF THE BANNERMAN FAMILY at Wyastone Leys, c. 1900 and 1907. The top photograph probably shows J.M. Bannerman with his three sons, John, Ronald and Robert. The photograph below is dated 1907, and shows three unidentified people playing diabola on the front lawn.

KING ARTHUR'S CAVE, 1870/71, during excavations which first revealed the importance of the two-chambered cave as an Upper Paleolithic shelter which also contained the bones of ice-age animals such as woolly rhinoceros, mammoth, hyena and cave lion. To uncover these remains, dynamite was used to remove a layer of concrete-like stalagmite deposit. In the photograph the rubble is being removed.

THE SEVEN SISTERS' ROCKS, c. 1900. The man in the coracle is fishing.

SYMONDS YAT, looking downstream with the station on the left, the Longstone above. The Ross-on-Wye and Monmouth Railway was opened in 1873 and closed to passengers in 1959. The station area is now used as a car park. A few remains of the station can be seen, including one of the supports for the overhanging shelter which is shown in the photograph (see opposite, below).

SYMONDS YAT STATION, (top) c. 1910, (below) 1904.

GREAT DOWARD FROM SYMONDS YAT EAST, C. 1890. The remains of the limestone quarries and kilns, now overgrown with trees, can be seen at the top of the hill.

THE FERRY SLIPWAY, Symonds Yat, c. 1873. The photograph seems to have been taken during construction of the railway, before the station was completed.

An Easy Win at Symond's Yat Regatta

REGATTA, Symonds Yat, c. 1925. If the event was anything like earlier regattas it included canoe, punt and coracle races, as well as the coxed pair shown here.

SYMONDS YAT WEST from Huntsham Hill, C. 1870, the Ferry Inn buildings are in the centre.

THE WYE AT SYMONDS YAT, C. 1880, looking downstream from the west bank at the Ferry Inn.

COLDWELL ROCKS, C. 1880, from the cottages below the Yat Rock. The sign over the door of the nearest building reads: 'Joseph Mathews. Lemonade. Gingerade. Tea Parties Supplied.' The railway line can be seen in the valley bottom, having just emerged from the Symond's Yat tunnel.

COLDWELL ROCKS, C. 1880.

LYDBROOK VIADUCT, c. 1900. The foundation stone was laid on 9 November 1872. The work was carried out by the Crumlin Viaduct Works Co. The viaduct linked the Severn and Wye Railway system in the Forest of Dean with the Ross and Monmouth Railway at Lydbrook Junction. It was demolished in the 1960s.

WELSH BICKNOR, c. 1870. The Church of St Margaret was built in 1858/9.

THE WYE JUST DOWNSTREAM FROM KERNE BRIDGE. The bridge in the distance carried the Ross – Monmouth railway. Bicknor railway tunnel is on the right of the bridge, which no longer exists, although one of the embankments leading to it has been converted into a viewing platform and information point.

KERNE BRIDGE, looking north from Coppet Hill. The remains (refectory) of the Augustinian Priory of Flanesford are on the left. On the right of the bridge the Ross – Monmouth Railway is either under construction or very newly completed (1873). Kerne Bridge itself was erected in 1828.

RIGHT: GOODRICH CASTLE, 1869. The fine square keep, seen in the top photograph, was built in the mid-twelfth century and is the earliest surviving part of the castle. On the left of the keep is one of the three projecting circular corner towers of the late-thirteenth century, when the castle was almost completely rebuilt. The bottom photograph shows the entrance gate, looking from the D-shaped barbican which was added to the new defences in around 1320. There is a strong contrast between the overgrown and crumbling ruins shown and the castle as it is presented today.

GOODRICH COURT, three views, c. 1870. Built in 1828 by Edward Blore for Sir Samuel Meyrick to house his renowned collection of armour, the mock castle was designed to mirror its neighbour the real Goodrich Castle, and attracted Wordsworth's displeasure as a piece of architecture. It was demolished just after the Second World War, leaving only its gatehouse, skirted by the dual-carriageway of the A40. In 1893, the *Beacon* reported on the installation of electricity at the house, by this time owned by H.C. Moffat. The power was supplied by two oil engines, lighting 250 lamps, the light of which was 'remarkably steady and brilliant . . . a marked contrast to the gas and oil formerly in use.' Control of the four switchboards was in the sole charge of the butler, while the estate carpenter was entrusted with the engines. The photograph, top left, shows the Court from Goodrich Castle. On this page is a view of the smoking-room.

LOWER REDBROOK, the timber and shipbuilding yard, c. 1880. Shipbuilding was carried out at Redbrook in the first half of the nineteenth century, although the narrowness of the river restricted the size of the products, which were mainly barges and trows.

THE VILLAGE INSTITUTE, Redbrook, probably just after erection in 1886. It was built at the expense of the Tinplate Company, by C. Morgan of May Hill, Monmouth. The crowd is probably of tinplate workers, including, to judge from appearances, managers and perhaps directors.

UPPER REDBROOK, showing the Wye Valley Flour Mills (see over) and, in the smoke, the tramway incline, part of the Monmouth to Coleford tramway of 1812, which linked the Upper and Lower Redbrook ironworks to the main tramline.

ANSLEY'S MILL, Upper Redbrook, 1877. Ansley was a brewer who lived opposite the mill, which was a corn and grist mill and may also have been part of Coster's ironworks.

WYE VALLEY FLOUR MILLS, Upper Redbrook. The Courteen family owned and ran the mill until just after the First World War. A Henry Courteen, miller, is recorded in Redbrook in 1811. In 1873, the mill was reopened, after re-building the structure shown in the photograph. The mill was destroyed by fire in 1925.

MILLERS AND CARTERS AT THE WYE VALLEY FLOURMILLS, c. 1880.

REDBROOK BREWERY, c. 1905. The brewery premises were demolished in 1926. The photograph has been dated on the evidence of the headgear worn by most of those present, which looks like the surplus army helmets sold off by the Government after the Boer War. We have no information about the event or the people shown.

THE TINPLATE WORKS, Lower Redbrook, c. 1900. The production of tinplate at Lower Redbrook began in 1771 and continued until 1961.

MR. HAROLD WHITEHOUSE, furnaceman at the tinplate works, shown on the way to work in around 1934. The white apron and the clean white towel around the neck were hallmarks of the 'mill man'.

TINPLATE WORKERS, Redbrook Tinplate Works. The top photograph, shows sheets of iron ready for processing on the right. It is undated but certainly before the First World War. Note the long-handled tongs of the furnacemen on the left. Below are the younger men and boys of the 'tin house', or 'wash house', in around 1920.

TINPLATE WORKERS, Redbrook Siding, August 1961. Steel bars, the raw material, arrived at the sidings and the finished tinplates departed from there to all parts of the world. This was the last consignment of steel to be unloaded before the works closed.

'BIG MILL', Redbrook Tinplate Works, 1961. Mr Anthony Philpotts rolling the last steel bar before closure. Mill men were usually dressed in grey flannel collarless shirts which were short-sleeved, vented at the sides and worn outside the trousers. Note the protective sleeve on the forearm. Newspaper is tied over the toe-cap of the left boot.

THE DIRECTORS OF THE REDBROOK TINPLATE CO., 1916, after a board meeting at the Beaufort Hotel, Tintern. Left to right: Alexander Taylor (managing director); Joseph Coventry (chairman); H.J. Milner (secretary); A.F. Robinson; J.C. Robinson; Ernest Coventry.

REDBROOK ASSOCIATION FOOTBALL CLUB, winners of the *Beacon* cup, 1934/5 season. Back row, left to right: (committee) F. Pick; W.L. Bevan (hon. sec. and trainer); L. Hudson; S. Horton (president); J. Hughes (chairman); S. Gill; T. Hudson (treasurer); W. Hudson. Front row, left to right: (players): M. Evans; N. Hawkins; A. Whitehouse; J. Lee; J. Golder; S. Cutter (capt.); W. Price; H. Fletcher; M. Butler; R. Morgan; A. Beech.

ABOVE: THE WEDDING OF MAY BEARD, Redbrook, c. 1914. She was the daughter of the manager of the Tinplate Works, Edwin Beard, seen here sitting to the left of the bride. The groom was Mr Teague.

TOP, LEFT: THE WYE AT LOWER REDBROOK, showing the Wye Valley Railway, opened in 1876. The photograph was taken before the small halt on the line for Penallt was opened in 1931 (see below).

LEFT: UNLOADING BEER, PENALLT HALT, September 1959. The beer was for The Boat at Penallt. Ted Morgan, porter, is on the left with Arthur Chandler, guard.

LLANDOGO, looking upstream, c. 1900. In the foreground is the Wye Valley railway, with Railway Cottage on the left. In the eighteenth and early-nineteenth centuries the village was a centre for the processing and export of timber from the surrounding hills, producing oak bark, chair legs, broom-handles, hoops and staves for barrel-making and boats. There is now no trace of the shipbuilding industry, and no clue as to where the work actually took place.

A SIMILAR VIEW to the one opposite, c. 1910 but showing two trows moored on the beach of the Gloucester bank, one of them reputedly called the *George and Mary*.

LLANDOGO, from the Monmouth to Chepstow road, constructed in 1828. The Church of St Oudoceus was opened in 1861 and restored in 1889.

BROCKWEIR, looking downstream before the construction of the road bridge in 1906. With its boatbuilding industry and barge trade, Brockweir had a definite maritime character in the eighteenth and early-nineteenth centuries, with a quayside and, apparently, 16 pubs in 1820.

RIGHT: THE CONSTRUCTION OF BROCKWEIR BRIDGE, by Finch & Co. of Chepstow. The top photograph shows the girders as they arrived by barge (see over). They were lifted into place by steam powered winches (below).

ABOVE: GIRDERS FOR BROCKWEIR BRIDGE arriving by barge from Finch & Co., Chepstow (see previous page).

TOP, RIGHT: BROCKWEIR from the Monmouth–Chepstow road, before construction of the bridge, showing two trows moored.

RIGHT: *'LA BELLE MARIE'*, Brockweir, a twin-screwed steamboat of 31 tons which was used on the Wye from Brockweir by Mr James Dibden before the First World War. Her remains were uncovered at the quayside in 1967.

THE FERRY CROSSING, Brockweir. The construction of the bridge marked the end of the ferry, previously the only way to cross the river, and particularly lucrative for the owner when the Wye Valley railway was opened. A court case was fought over the issue at the time the bridge was being built.

THE MORAVIAN CHAPEL SUNDAY SCHOOL, August 1912. Founded in 1833 in default of any Church of England presence in the then busy port, the church was revived in the 1960s through links with Monmouth Baptist Church. So far, none of the people in the picture have been named.

FOUR VIEWS OF BROCKWEIR c. 1905. From the top left, they are titled: Cottage and Children; Girl Sweeping Outside Cottage; Carrying Water; The Mill Stream.

MONMOUTH BUILDING WORKERS, c. 1905. The group includes members of the main trades necessary to erect a building: mason, carpenter, decorator, and assorted labourers. However, although several names are scribbled on the back (Yearsley, Ward, Watkins, Davies), exact identities and the reason for the photograph are not yet known.

ACKNOWLEDGEMENTS

Mrs Adlam • Mrs G. Alsop • Mrs B. Ballinger • J. Barry • Mr C. Bigham
Cllr W. Blake • Mrs Blake • Mrs E. Boulton • S. Bowe • Mrs A.M. Bowen
Mr G. Bundy • Mr Bywater • Mr W.A. Call • Mr S.H. Clarke • Mr F.W. Collins
Mrs P.G. Croudace • Mrs D. Croudace • Mr E.T. Davies • Mr H. Davies
Mr Day • Mrs Dunford • Mr D. Edwards • Mr R. Elias • J.W. Elliott
Capt. N.C. Elstob • Mr R. Ferneyhough • E. Finch & Co., Chepstow
Mrs Frost • Mr P. Gimmonds • Col. J.C.E. Harding • Mr P.G. Harris • T. Harris
Mrs Hayward • Mr W. Higgins • Mr K. Howell • Dr E. Horton • Mr G.C. Hughs
Mrs Hunt • Miss R. Jenkins • Mrs Jones • Mrs Kirby • Mrs A. Kissack
Mr K.E. Kissack • Mr P. Landon • A.R. Lane • B. Lewis • Monmouth Baptist
Church • Mrs E.L. Morris • Mr J. Page • Mr & Mrs Payne • Mrs H.M. Payton
Mr R.W. Pearce • Mr A. Philpotts • Dr Potter • Mrs L.M. Powell • Mr F. Pyner
Miss K. Reade • Mr Rickards • P. Simmonds • Mr B. Stevens • Mr Snoop
Mr Tippins • Miss M. Vile • Mrs M. Walsh • Mr D. Waters • Mr M.P. Watkins
Mr D.G. Webb • M. Weaving • Mrs D. Whitehouse • Mr J. Wigmore
Miss B. Williams • Mr M. Worrall.